Tears of the Soul

Eric Moore

PublishAmerica
Baltimore

First printing

At the specific preference of the author, PublishAmerica allowed this work to remain exactly as the author intended, verbatim, without editorial input.

ISBN: 1-4241-1407-1
PUBLISHED BY PUBLISHAMERICA, LLLP
www.publishamerica.com
Baltimore

Printed in the United States of America

Dedication and Acknowledgments

First of all I would like to give all praise and glory to my Lord and savior. Without his infinite wisdom and grace I would not be here to share my soul with my readers. They say when you don't use a gift or talent, the Lord will take it away. I hope that this small token is using my God given talent.

Next I would love to thank my family. My grandmother Diane Moore, who has pushed and is even now still pushing me to be better than I think I can be. Thank you Gammy. My mother, Dee Moore, who tells me that I am a good person no matter what anyone tells me. Thank you for being a mother and father to me. My aunties, Debra Moore and Denise Kaigler, who keep me grounded when I seem to be floating off into outer space and not taking care of my priorities and responsibilities. And finally my brother Eron Moore, my sisters DeAndra and KaRhonda Moore, my cousins, nephews and my nieces. Its so good to have a family that I can trust and love. Thank you all.

Finally I would like to thank two women that will always have my heart and soul. Women that I see every night that I dream. Two women that are every word I write and every tear that I cry. Those women are my beautiful daughter Azari and her wonderful mother Tessa. Without these outstanding women, I never would have truly found "great love." So to you, know that I love you so very much, and can't wait to hold you in my arms again.

"True love is not when the heart beats faster or fastest, it's when the heart beats no more and the love is still there. True love is constancy and submission. "

Contents

Introduction

SOUL

1. nonphysical aspect of person: the complex of human attributes that manifests as consciousness, thought, feeling, and will, regarded as distinct from the physical body
2. religion spirit surviving death: in some systems of religious belief, the spiritual part of a human being that is believed to continue to exist after the body dies.
The soul is sometimes regarded as subject to future reward and punishment, and sometimes as able to take a form that allows it to remain on or return to earth.
3. feelings: somebody's emotional and moral nature, where the most private thoughts and feelings are hidden

MAN

1. an adult male human being.
2. virile person: the personification of qualities traditionally associated with the male sex, including courage, strength, and aggression, or somebody with such qualities.

The soul of a man is deep and often misunderstood. As a man I know this first hand and can say that women today see many things, want many things, and dream of many things, that their mates must possess before they step into a serious relationship. What bugs me is that women say that a man has no heart. But isn't it a woman that also says that the way to a man's heart is through his stomach. I don't get it. Why contradict a phrase when you yourselves as women don't want to take the time to find out if that man has a heart, or more importantly has a soul. That leads me to believe, that more women than men are heartless and soulless. A time comes to mind when all was good with the opposite sexes. We played, we had fun, we did everything with one another. I'm a young man and so that time wasn't to long ago. But what ever happened to that time? What ever happened to romance, affection, commitment. I wonder what ever happened to just being yourself and looking for the right man or right woman. Instead we all seem to looking for, excuse my use of an overly used phrase, Mister or Misses 'Right Now.'

I have been in relationships, dated, and had my occasional one-night stands. But with the exception of those few one-niters, I have always gotten to know my mates. A few I have even said 'I love you' too. So why is it not important now, to get to know your man or woman before you make that jump head first into a relationship? We all have done it at some time or another, maybe even on a subconscious level. But is has been done with us all. So my question to all the men and women in the world is this. What does it take for a good man to be the man that a good woman really needs?

I know what the women reading this are saying. What about us? Doesn't a man deserve a good woman? Yes we do deserve a good woman. But the thing about that is, women tend to put all emotions on the line when they do get into a relationship. As do real good men. Why try to hide what will eventually come out anyways. But when a woman does that it sends a sign to a man that she is vulnerable. And be it a good man or a misguided fool of a man. Everything that that man may say or do is magnified a million fold. So whatever is done, even done in a jokingly manner, a woman in that state of mind will view it as being sarcastic, hypocritical, or even consider that man to be lying or covering up something in his past or his present. Which in turn will get her to thinking and assuming. And we all know what that does in the end. So women, its not that you don't deserve a good man, its the fact that you may have a good man right now and you are taking his love as something else. We want to play with you, we want to love you like you want to be loved. But ladies, let us be us. We try and try, just as you will try and try. But we a men know what we want. And when that comes along we try everything to keep that relationship intact and growing.

ROMANTIC

1. involving sexual love: involving or characteristic of a love affair or sexual love, especially when the relationship is idealized or exciting and intense
2. suitable for love: characterized by or suitable for lovemaking or the expression of tender emotions
3. involving enthusiasm: relating to or characterized by a fascination or enthusiasm for something, especially of an uncritical or indefinable kind

Now that is a word that so many people use, but don't even know the true definition of. What you have above is what Webster and all the other dictionaries say romantic means. But of course the true meaning you are about to learn. The true

11

meaning of romantic is a man or woman that is caring, loving, thoughtful, and has the ability to learn and adapt to their mate. By that I mean whatever you have going on in your relationship, be it problems or situations, you as a romantic can take them in stride and work them out without drama or complications. See I consider myself as a 'helpless romantic', whereas I do whatever possible to make my woman as happy as she deserves and then some. I do all the things that it takes to make a serious committed relationship work. And after all that is done or being worked on, I write a little note in a card with some flowers and send it directly to her place of employment or at her home. I also cook for my woman. Yes ladies, some men do know how to cook a good meal, in my case a great meal is only a few hours away. See I try to do all the little things that go along with being in a happy relationship. But there are those times when there can be no happy relationship.

And that is where most people end. In an unhappy relationship! They spend two years together, and don't know the single most important thing about their opposites. Don't know what he or she likes for breakfast. Don't even know where their mates work at or what their schedules are. How can you be in a relationship when you don't even know when you will be seeing one another. People you have to ask questions to find out what your man or woman wants. You have to talk in order to know what your man or woman needs. And most importantly, you have to take that journey to the center of their souls, to see if that man or woman is the right man or woman for you!

RELATIONSHIPS

1. connection: a significant connection or similarity between two or more things, or the state of being related to something else
2. behavior or feelings toward somebody else: the connection between two or more people or groups and their involvement with each other, especially as regards how they behave and feel toward each other and communicate or cooperate

Relationships, now there is a word that most men and woman cringe at when spoken. Its not the word itself, but the work that is involved with the word. Not saying that it is a great deal of work just to start a relationship, but is a lot of work to maintain one. Relationships tend to get messier as the time goes on with the two. The arguments get stronger. The nights get lonelier. And yes even the sex starts to go south. But what is it that makes relationships go bad? First lets go with the women. What can they do to make their relationships last longer?

1. Women you can stop bringing up or comparing your current boyfriend with the mistakes former ones have made or what they did to what he does now. Two different people, two different relationships.
2. Women you should quit trying to make one man into multiple men. That said, if you don't like what you have, and never did. Why are you there in the first place?
3. When a problem arises, don't just run from it, stay and work it out. What doesn't kill you, can only make you stronger. And keep you and your man happier.
4. Stop getting into relationships just for the sex. You'll get it regardless of who you are in a relationship with. You should

kill two birds with one stone. Have the great sex with a good man too.

Now men, I know that we can sometimes be judged prematurely. But we do that to ourselves. We as men need to be consistent with our women. We need to make each and everyone feel like a princess or goddess. I know there are some fools out there that think woman are to be used and not loved. But for the rest of us, we don't have to give in to that stereotype. We can find love. We can be loved. We can make love till no one is left on the planet. But we must stay *romantically consistent.* So here gentlemen is what we as men can do to make our relationships last and last.

1. First off we can be ourselves. There are to many of us willing to change for a woman, just to find that they are not the right one or that that just isn't you. By that time its way too late to change back.
2. We as men have to be the shoulder for the woman to cry on. We have to be a friend and not just a lover. Its not wrong for us to be sensitive. Its not gay to sit down with your woman and just talk.
3. As a man, I have to make sure that my woman is first priority (behind God). Don't put her off to spend 3 days a week with your boys. Don't work all the time, neglecting your woman for days on end. Take care of her, love her. AND SHOW HER THAT YOU DO!!!
4. Same as #3 for the ladies. We have to stop running from relationships and there problems. They teach us. And believe me some of us need to learn.
5. Be a man!

See without rules there is no role. In a relationship everybody in it has his or her own role to play in it. And for that role to be played right, there must be rules involved. So set the foundation for your relationship. And try not to build something that is unorganized or backwards (i.e. don't put the roof on the house before the foundation is fully set). It will last so much longer for it.

Now the reason for this book is simple. To let everybody know, especially the women in the world, that there are some good men out there. And for you the see that you have to look deeper than the man's clothes, car, house and job. You have to take a simple look into his eyes, and follow the path to his soul. There you will see that a man is just as vulnerable as you are if not more. We get hurt just as much as women do. We hold on to memories just like women do. And yes, we fall hard in love, just like women do. So for all the real women, and all the real men, here is the book that tells every women what every real good man wants to say. So read on and I hope that you enjoy every piece of my soul that I have put into it. So to my fellas, read, learn and tell the woman of your dreams that you are so in love with them—and mean it with every bit of your soul.

First Night

Returning from heaven,
A task that seemed harder than it was,
Took a moment,
That seemed like eternity,
But will always remain permanent in my soul,
Each moment like a snapshot of ecstasy,
Each kiss playing over in my mind,
Our first night envisioned from the start,
Made closer with every stare,
Every embrace,
And creeping closer with every unspoken word,
That night,
Seemingly endless,
Intertwined intoxicated hearts,
Made one,
Of two yearning souls,
I awake to your presence,
Still dreaming that dream of passion,
Still thirsting for your nectar of lust,
My body conversing with your own,
Our eyes speaking languages foreign to our ears,
You're heaven sent,
My perfect angel,
That gave me last night,
That gave me,
Our first night.

_ _ _ n Come True

I'm a dreamer,
Ambitious,
Untiring in my own delusions,
But you are a dream,
My dream,
My only dream come true,
The subject of all my thoughts,
The passion in all my words,
Never imagined I would find you,
But dreamed of you my entire life,
Saw you since the first breath I took,
You are a dream,
My dream,
My only dream come true,
Hot days,
Turning into starry nights,
While starry skies,
Turn into refreshing mornings,
But will reality soon set in,
Will dreams keep playing over again,
Will you just be that lone figment,
Churning slowly,
Running always,
In the depths of my mind,
Now I see why we dream,
Because great dreams,
Do come true.

Discoveries

Just starting to discover all of you,
Just beginning to discover my true self,
But when things are new,
Discovery is something that we all must do,
It's great to learn,
What your inside holds,
What makes you tick,
What makes you tock,
What it is that makes you breath,
What it is that makes you think,
Great minds discovering glorious new things,
You and I beginning a life of golden rings,
Never tarnished,
Never fading,
Just lasting for all our lives,
What we discover,
Is what we have,
An eternity of one another,
Years of hand holding,
Deep kissing,
And lasting embraces,
So whatever I discover,
There's one thing that will never be new,
That one thing,
Is discovering,
How much I do love you.

Inexperienced

I'm fighting feelings,
I've never had before,
Scared of an outcome,
That I do not want,
You've given me new life,
Shown me new emotions,
I've given you an heir to our name,
My heart unconditionally,
We've bonded like nothing I have ever seen,
A short period of time,
Started a great thing,
That one great romance,
Read about in all the books,
But is it true,
Do you feel the same feelings I feel,
Know the same love I know,
And yearn for me,
Like I,
Yearn for you,
Never made a promise,
That I could not keep,
Never loved a woman,
Like I love you so deep,
In the grand scheme of things,
You are that one great love,
You're passion surrounding me,
You're love engulfing my soul,
My mind teetering,
On the cusp of obsession,
See you have me like this,

Tangled in a web of sweet kisses,
In unspoken conversations,
I feel you,
Your soul wrapped in my everything,
I see you,
While I sleep,
While I think,
I see you,
When I'm awake,
And you are not even near,
See yes,
I am fighting feelings,
That I never had,
A fight,
I very well might lose,
But a fight,
I would love to win.

What Does a Woman See First in a Man?

When looking at the outer appearance, women usually notice a man's physique first then the details that compliment his physical attraction. Then depending on the women doing the observing, she looks for patterns in his attitude, mood and looks for attributes in his character.

Day G. 25
Atlanta, GA

The first thing that I look at is the man's shoes. That tells a lot about a person's appearance. I also look at the man's fingernails and his teeth.

Deneshia W. 25
Thomaston, GA

What a woman first sees in a man is his pride and the way that he carries himself.

Seneca H. 24
Orangeburg, SC

I would say their personality. Important because it shows how they treat people as a whole.

Queneshia S. 19
Athens, GA

Personally I look for what's in their eyes.

Unknown Female

Different for every woman . First I check out the face, then how he is dressed. I then look at his shoes, hands and teeth.

Erica C. 19
Atlanta, GA

She looks at if he is sexy or not, plain and simple.

Dingarka J. 28
Brooklyn, NY

A woman looks for maturity and/or immaturity.

Joey S. 24
Jackson, MS

His attitude and how he treats the people around him (co-workers, friends, family and strangers). Also his sense of humor.

Rachel A. 33
Vancouver, WA

Lucky Me

It was just by chance,
That we were introduced,
Not face to face,
But by words,
Like a book,
A picture says a thousand words,
Also tells a million stories,
But it was just by chance,
That we were introduced,
Chance encounters,
Often end in grief,
But this,
Yes this,
Will have that fairy tale end,
I promise to love you,
Respect you,
Treat you like the queen you are,
The woman I vow to honor,
Protect,
Love through sickness and health,
Till the end of our days,
You're more than just perfect,
You're the greatest of the great,
My wife to be,
So I'm the lucky one,
That just by chance,
You were introduced to me.

Promises

I promise to love you,
Promise to adore,
I promise to satisfy,
Your each and every desire,
Promise to kiss you goodnight,
Promise to ask about your day,
Yes I promise,
Promise to make love to you,
In each and every way,
Promise to talk to you,
Promise to hold you,
This is me,
And I promise to touch you,
In just the right spot,
I'm going to promise my life,
Till the very end of time,
Promise that every Valentine,
I ask you to be mine,
With every promise that I make,
I'll love you more and more,
The best thing to happen to me,
Only want what you deserve,
Everything you dream,
Everything you fantasize,
Me in your life,
This I cannot lie,
This I promise you,
Till the day that I die.

Quiet Storm

When the rain falls,
The thunder roars,
And the lightening flashes,
I take that grand journey,
To the center of your soul,
And with a passionate kiss,
Our bodies dance to the rhythm of the rain,
Moving methodically to that sensual beat,
With every clasp of thunder,
I plunge deeper into your innocence,
You yearning to feel me through and through,
The night gets longer,
The rain falls harder,
But still we dance,
And still we move to that lustful beat,
Staring,
Gazing,
Into one another's hearts,
Lightening illuminating bare bodies,
As they become one,
Bodies glistening,
From that night's passion,
Glowing from the ecstasy we shared,
Loving every moment of the storm,
Not the thunder storm out of our world,
But our storm,
The storm we've made,
Our little quiet storm.

Is it Always Necessary to Use a Pick-up Line on a Woman?

No it is not necessary to use a pick-up line. Personality says it all. But some men do need pick-up lines.

Deneshia W. 22
Thomaston, GA

No, because I wouldn't want a guy to use the same line on me that he uses on everyone else. That would not make me feel like I am special to him.

Queneshia S. 19
Athens, GA

Not at all, Unless it is something just so romantic.

Unknown Female

Sometimes. But the truth is the best pick-up line there is.

Unknown Female

No not so much. I think that they are so corny and predictable.

Cicely B. 26
Savannah, GA

No you don't. Most pick-up lines are cheesy. Most guys that use them on me get brushed off, unless they make me laugh.

Erica C. 19
Atlanta, GA

No, pick-up lines are insulting. Just be yourself.

Stacy M. 30-something
Providence, RI

Not at all. To be completely honest, in my experiences, the woman usually uses the pick-up line first.

Dingarka J. 28
Brooklyn, NY

Not at all. Your demeanor and your personality with a nice hello and a warm smile is all most women need.

Rachel A. 33
Vancouver, WA

Real Man

If you look in my eyes,
You'll see I'm a real man,
Been through a lot of things,
Been fighting as hard as I can,
I am a real man,
Cried for most of my life,
I am a real man,
Have loved and lost,
But throughout my ordeals,
All through my negative past,
I've stood as a man,
Stayed fighting as hard as I can,
No one can tell me,
You weren't good at this,
No one can ever say,
You weren't to small to do that,
For me to sit by,
And not do a thing,
Wouldn't be who I am,
wouldn't even feel the same
So when you look in my eyes,
Tell me what do you see,
Do you see a dark outline,
Or a clear image of me,
I'll tell you what you see,
There's no answer that I need,
You see a real man,
Who's been working,
A man who's free,
You've spotted a man who dreams,

Who wants all the wealth in the world,
Not money,
Or gold,
Silver,
Or pearls,
Just knowledge,
And happiness,
Are all that I need,
So just think to yourself,
Who that masked man is,
He's a man who cries,
A man who thinks,
A man who loves,
Oh yes,
I'm a man who dreams,
So sit back relax,
And think very hard,
If you want a man,
That fights as hard as he can,
Then I'm the one you need,
Because he's a real man.

One Moment

Just dreaming about you,
Will never be enough,
Seeing you,
Will only tease my soul,
Because nothing,
Not nothing,
Brings joy to me,
Like holding you,
For just one moment,
Feeling your heart beat against my own,
Having my thoughts come to life,
My fantasy fulfilled,
And my whole life changed,
By holding you,
For just one moment,
I can make love to you,
Every night of our lives,
Kiss you,
Every chance I get,
But one simple act,
One simple sign of affection,
Makes everything so right,
Makes me so complete,
So with everything that I can do,
And everything I have done,
All I need,
Is to hold you,
Just one time,
For just one moment.

When Is the Right Time to Say "I Love You" to Your Man or Woman?

After time, when love has been tested. The word love is not even used as sacred as it used to be used before and has somehow lost it's essence.

Day G. 25
Atlanta, GA

Whenever you feel that you do love them. No need to play games, if you feel it then you feel it.

Deneshia W. 22
Thomaston, GA

The right time to tell your man or woman that you love them, is when you both have established that understanding that you both can't live without one another.

Seneca H. 24
Orangeburg, SC

I say I love you when I mean it. Also when I know for sure that the other person is feeling the same. But that person loving you back does not always happen, so I may never say I love you.

Unknown Female

When you know that you are in love with them. Tell them when the mood and the time is right.

Joey S. 24
Jackson, MS

At least 3 months into the relationship. AND NOT DURING
SEX!!!!!

Cicely B. 26
Savannah, GA

At the earliest 3 months. Anything earlier, I wont believe it. But
the common rule is 3 months.

Erica C. 19
Atlanta, GA

When you know the feeling is true. You should never deny
yourself the opportunity to experience that emotion. You never
know if that person feels the same about you.

Unknown Female

Reflection

My mind is clear,
Just thoughts about you,
My soul is pure,
Filled only with love for you,
My heart is strong,
Knowing that you will come back to me,
Decisions made that are the best for you,
But decisions made,
That hurt so much,
My mistakes,
My problems,
My life,
Too much to handle,
I tried,
But still,
I must try some more,
Put my biggest foot forward,
Put everything into each word,
Each kiss,
Place everything I have,
Into you,
My mind is clear,
Just thinking of you,
My soul is pure,
Filled with only the love,
I still have for you.

3rd Person

There's no need to cry,
Just be who you are,
There's no need to quit,
Just be yourself,
There's no need to be anything,
But the man that she sees,
Romantic,
Secure,
Poetic and more,
You have what they need,
You just want the one you lost,
Yes you have what they want,
Women of every shade,
Race,
And creed,
You'll always have what they want,
But still it's her that you need,
Like a lock of Samson's hair,
She's your confidence,
Your strength,
She's the air you breath,
So there's no need to cry,
Just be who you are,
Yes you have what they want,
But its only her that you need.

My Thoughts

Just sitting here thinking,
About the times we shared,
Some good,
Some bad,
But in any situation.
Together is what we were,
There have been those spots,
That were rougher than most,
Still we got through them,
Persevered,
Came out,
Stronger than before,
So I am just sitting here thinking,
Can we do it once more,
See I've said some things,
That I wish I never spoke,
I'm young,
A little foolish,
And I love you so much,
Just needed a little time,
To figure it out,
Who you are,
Who I am,
And what we can become,
A love that is strong,
Is immortal,
And should not die,
See,
I'm just sitting here thinking,
Hoping you feel the same way I do,

I sit away,
Depressed,
Lonely,
Sit away hoping,
Wishing,
If you could,
If you would,
Bring your kiss back to me,
Just bring your love back,
Back to my open arms,
Back into my life,
A new man,
With a new attitude,
But wanting that same love,
That same woman,
That same you,
Just sitting here thinking,
About the times we shared,
Some good,
Some bad,
But in any situation,
Together is what we were,
And together is where we belong.

What Is the First Thing a Man Sees in a Woman?

Always physical, so its the way that woman carries herself.

Erica C. 19
Atlanta, GA

Depends on the man, if he can really see her, then I would say her eyes, smile, looks or her body.

Jackie

Her smile and part of the part of the body he is most attracted to.

Rachel A. 33
Vancouver, WA

For some its what lies behind her smile.

Unknown Female

Don't Care Anymore

You wanted to know,
Yet I still cant tell,
Not that I'm scared,
But only because,
You now don't care,
Our souls blackened by hate,
How dare you love me,
Care for you,
Kiss me,
Then leave,
Leave me alone,
To fend for myself,
To my pillow,
And wish it was you,
Wish was the woman I longed to have,
Why did you go,
What did I do,
What did I say,
To make you leave,
Couldn't help but love you,
You were everything to me,
I cant believe its over,
Angry to see it go,
My heart stopped beating,
The moment my world crashed,
The second my soul died,
I needed you to love me,
To care for me,
Kiss me,
To always be there for me,

I hate this so much,
don't know what to do,
My emotions all tangled as one,
My heart ceasing to beat,
It hurts,
It hurts so bad,
Hurts more than air,
Being ripped from my lungs,
I don't know what to do,
See you wanted to know,
Yet everything I still cant tell,
Not that I'm scared,
But only because you now don't care,
Don't care anymore,
Cant believe,
You now don't care.

Plans

We're still together,
Our love is still strong,
We've planned to be together,
For days past eternity,
Planned to be there for our children,
There for each other,
Plans made to just be there,
All our plans,
Up in smoke,
Engulfed by the fire,
That were our words,
We planned so much,
Our future so set in stone,
Just meant to be,
But plans and promises broken,
Erased,
Lost in translation,
From our first kiss,
To our last argument,
I loved you,
And yes,
You loved me,
My life unfulfilled,
Unplanned,
Incomplete,
We've planned to be together,
For days past eternity,
We did have,
A lifetime of plans.

I Knew

I just knew,
The first time,
The very first time I held your hand,
I knew right then,
The first time our lips touched,
I cant remember,
A single moment,
When you weren't on my mind,
When I didn't want to hold you,
Want to kiss you,
When everything confusing,
Became so crystal clear,
After that first night with you,
My life so great,
With you by my side,
On my arm,
And in my soul,
My angel,
Here on earth,
The greatest love that I'll ever know,
All mine,
To spoil,
To caress,
To treat like the queen she deserves to be,
The first time I held your hand,
I knew,
Knew you were the only one,
The only one for me.

Is Sex the First Thought When Trying to Approach a Man or Woman?

No it doesn't. I am wondering if he will reject me, accept me or even have the time to be able to deal with me.

Cicely B. 26
Savannah, GA

It depends on what that person is looking for. Who you are approaching and what you are approaching for.

Erica C. 19
Atlanta, GA

No it does not, but there must be some type of physical attraction between the two.

Stacy M. 30-something
Providence, RI

Not just sexual, but the knowledge of whether or not we are willing to have a physical relationship with a person can be determined in the first meeting.

Unknown Female

These days, with the subliminal and pressures of the media, TV, music videos, movies and etc. I believe that it is a thought of the subconscious. So I have heard from some men.

Day G. 25
Atlanta

No sex isn't the first thought I think about when approaching a man. The very first thing in my mind when approaching a man is whether he is able to cater to my needs.

Seneca H. 24
Orangeburg, SC

Not right off the bat. Originally I am trying to get to know his background and his personality.

Queneshia S. 19
Athens, GA

Sex isn't the first thought in my mind, but I am thinking is sex the first thing on his mind. Will he be a stalker? Also will he be a waste of time?

Unknown Female

By the Time

By the time you read this,
My love will have grown another bound,
My heart beat a thousand times,
And my mind thought of you,
For the millionth minute,
Thought about those mesmerizing eyes,
Which captured a child's soul,
Released it as a man's true love,
Those same eyes,
That brought a real romantic,
Down to one knee,
Not only to proclaim his love for forever and a day,
But to signify the perfection that he has witnessed,
Those same thoughts,
Reminiscing about every kiss,
Every embrace,
And every time we shared one another,
I loser my breath,
When those thoughts cross my mind,
When I see you,
Touch you,
Even when I sleep,
So by the time you read this,
My love will have grown another bound,
My heart beat a thousand times,
And my mind thought of you,
For the millionth time,
Just by the time,
You read this.

Vanish

I want to leave,
Just vanish,
Become one with the universe,
Let life swallow me,
Get rid of all problems,
All situations,
Close of all things harmful to my world,
Yeah,
Just leave,
Vanish,
Let life swallow me whole,
I want to start over,
Turn a whole new page,
Begin a new chapter,
In this story we call life,
All my past,
Put deep in the dark,
No light,
No chance to escape,
My future just that,
Mine,
So maybe,
I do need to leave,
Vanish,
Become one with the universe,
Maybe,
Let life,
Swallow me whole.

End of the Day

At the end of the day,
I think about you,
All about you,
And only of you,
About there way you make me feel,
The way you touch me,
Both emotionally,
And physically,
Think about the way,
You look me in the eyes,
Take that journey,
To the center of my soul,
And know,
Just know,
Exactly what,
And how I'm feeling,
To have that,
Is what every person wants,
What every person yearns to own,
And to lose it,
To let it slip,
So far far away,
Is not just darkness,
But the end of my life,
So at the end of the day,
I think about you,
All about you,
And only of you,

Crystal Clear

No hidden meaning,
No secret agenda,
Just the words that come out of my mouth,
When I say that I respect you,
Respect is what I give,
If I say you can trust me,
Then my world is in your hands,
And yes,
Those magical three words,
Spoken when two universes join as one,
So clear,
As to allow the yellow rays of sunshine,
To pass through every black cloud,
So what I say,
Is what I mean,
Nothing false,
Nothing fake,
Nor an illusion to the soul,
I respect you,
Respect me,
I trust you,
Trust me,
And love me,
Like I love you,
With meaning,
And without secrets,
Make love,
So crystal clear.

Passion

Its that kiss,
So powerful and strong,
That just the touching of lips,
Causes the clouds to collide,
And the skies to open up,
The flash of lightening,
The pounding of thunder,
that's what you call Passion,
Its that touch of your hand,
So soft,
So gentle,
Just the thought,
Sends shivers through my body,
From the tips of my fingers,
Down the length of my spine,
Straight through,
To the core of my soul,
that's what you call Passion,
Its that look,
That one captivating look,
So mesmerizing in its stare,
That it turns a black heart,
Into brand new snow,
Innocent,
In its purest form,
As white as real love,
The realist of the real,
Now that's what you call Passion,
Real,
Fulfilling Passion.

What Are the Most Important Factors in a Relationship?

Trust
Communication
Honesty

Kandace F. 25
San Francisco, CA

Compatibility
Trust
Love
Compassion
Honesty
Attraction
Loyalty

Stacy M. 30-something
Providence, RI

Trust
Loyalty
Honesty

Dingarka J. 28
Brooklyn, NY

Devotion
Love
Trust
Honesty
Respect
Friendship

Jackie

Communication
Physical attraction
Shared interests

Cicely B. 25
Savannah, GA

Honesty
Support
Respect between the two
Ability to compromise

Erica C. 19
Atlanta, GA

Trust
Love
Respect
Humor

Rachel A. 33
Vancouver, WA

Trust
Responsibility
Love
Equality

Joey S. 24
Jackson, MS

Trust
Honesty
Integrity

JaQuinnia R. 19

Trust
Honesty
Quality time together

Unknown Female

Consistancy
Respect
Communication
Flexibility
Trust
Comfort
Intimacy

Unknown Female

Understanding
Goals
Boundaries
Purpose for the relationship
Communication
Progression
Understanding of both person's past

Day G. 25
Atlanta, GA

Trust
Honesty
Sharing
Understanding

Deneshia W. 22
Thomaston, GA

Trust
Honesty
Loyalty
Friendship
Commitment

Seneca H. 24
Orangeburg, SC

When Things Go Wrong

Why get mad,
when things go wrong,
They say,
What doesn't kill you,
Will only make you stronger,
So don't get mad,
Let the world do what it can,
Take what it gives you,
don't wilt,
Just become a man,
No more crying,
If things don't go your way,
No more whining,
When it hasn't been your day,
Just sit back,
Relax,
Take what it gives,
Cause they do say,
What doesn't kill you,
Will only make you strong,
Strong in mind,
Strong in heart,
Body,
And strong of soul,
Stronger than most,
Because people do get mad,
When things seem to go wrong,
Those lonely souls die,
For they couldn't be strong,
When the world went wrong.

A Woman's Man

From start to finish,
You're always there for her,
To hold her,
When things aren't right,
To talk,
And comfort her,
Until there is no more night,
You have to trust her,
Adore her,
Be the man that she needs,
Be the star of her fantasies,
The director of her dreams,
Respect her,
Treat her,
Like the queen she deserves to be,
Your that woman's man,
Her prince charming,
That knight in shining armor,
So hold her,
Caress her,
Treat her better than the rest,
So be there,
From start to finish,
Love her,
Like nothing else matters,
Be the man that she needs,
Cause you are,
That woman's man.

What Does a Woman's Soul Consist Of?

A woman's soul has love and compassion flowing freely through it's fibers.

Queneshia S. 19
Athens, GA

Emotions and a lot more emotions is what i think it consists of.

Unknown Female

A woman's soul has unparalleled strength, compassion, understanding and unconditional love.

Unknown Female

Her feelings and emotions, intellect, memories and imagination.

Day G. 25
Atlanta, GA

A woman's soul consist of power, compassion, love and integrity.

Deneshia W. 22
Thomaston, GA

God, Love, Empathy, Ambition, and Determination is what a real woman's soul consists of.

Unknown Female

A woman's soul consist of love, spirituality, beauty and empowerment.

Seneca H. 24
Orangegurg, SC

Deep emotional thought, wonder, luster and of course love is what engulfs a woman's soul.

JaQuinnia R. 19

The woman's soul consists of all things maternal and nurturing. Also has love, devotion and just a touch of jealousy.

Rachel A. 33
Vancouver, WA

What a woman's soul has in it depends on the woman and how many scars she has on her soul from her previous relationships.

Stay M. 30-something
Providence, RI

What a woman's soul consist of is pride, independence, love, truth, respect, living life to the fullest, trust, and loving herself as a person.

Jackie

Her feelings, her emotions, her compassion, true instincts, and her maternal instincts are what makes a woman's soul.

Cicely B. 26
Savannah, GA

A nurturing spirit, a very caring person, compassion and a lot of mushy stuff happens to be what is in my soul. And last time I checked I was a female.

Erica C. 19
Atlanta, GA

Superstar

I'm something beyond wonderment,
Possessing something,
Way past your understanding,
Having skills that label me,
Talents that haunt me,
Impressive is a word,
Used at first sight,
I'm just being myself,
An ailment capable of being terminal,
A fault that cannot be reversed,
I'm something beyond wonderment,
Possessing something,
Way past your understanding,
Mature beyond natural years,
Immortal in a land of dead souls,
Outlasting time itself,
Stumbling over nothing,
Soaring over all things,
Over all obstacles,
Life's paths never blocked,
Never closed,
I'm something beyond wonderment,
Possessing something,
Way past your understanding,
I'm on levels,
Never obtained before,
A pioneer for mankind,
Shooting past the farthest galaxy,
Exploring new reaches in the heavens,
A man among boys,

A king for all kings,
Placed here to spread my wealth,
To teach my thoughts,
I'm something beyond wonderment,
Just being the superstar that I am.

With You

I find myself thinking,
Wanting,
Hoping,
You were here with me,
Never felt like this,
A love that can be everlasting,
You're greatness staring me in the eyes,
Happiness knocking at the doorway to my soul,
Wouldn't wish this to end,
Couldn't wish you away,
My life so complete,
Just by knowing who you are,
The more I learn,
The more I need you,
Right here with me,
Growing old with me,
Loving me,
One man,
One heart,
A heart that yearns,
To beat alongside your own,
To hold you,
Caress you,
Kiss you,
For the rest of our lives,
For the long days past eternity,
Past forever,
But never past the love I have for you,
Never felt like this,
A love that can be everlasting,

You're greatness staring me in the eyes,
Happiness knocking at the doorway to my soul,
Wouldn't wish this to end,
Couldn't wish you away,
My life so complete,
Right now,
So very complete,
Just by being with you.

Worth Living

Around the corner,
There's problems to face,
Down the block a bit,
Storms are forming,
Ready to rain on your success,
But through all that,
Life's peaches and cream,
A piece of cake,
Through all the trials and tribulations,
Life is worth living,
Worth living to its fullest,
Time to carpe the whole diem,
Don't leave a minute wasted,
Let no second be forgotten,
Turn over every hour,
Just to live this thing,
We call life,
You cant hide from it,
There's nowhere to run,
Life is all around you,
Smothering you,
Engulfing,
Through all its trials,
All its tribulations,
Life is worth living,
Worth living to its fullest,
Worth living indeed.

What Is the Difference Between a Man Approaching a Woman, and a Woman Approaching a Man?

A man approaching a woman shows a man's confidence, which can be found to be very attractive. A woman approaching a man can sometimes be misunderstood as a woman who may have dominating tendencies versus the truth of just wanting to have an experience with a person she is intrigued by.

Unknown Female

The difference is that it is more traditional for the man to approach the woman. Whereas when the woman approaches the man, she is viewed as being either un-lady like (androgynous; we call it gender psychology) or too aggressive. That may even scare off or turn off the man that she is approaching. It brings the reverse role affect.

Day G. 25
Atlanta, GA

I think it is so romantic for a man to approach a woman, as long as it is done in a respectful manner. But if I see something that I like, I don't mind going after it. Its very rare, but I will.

Unknown Female

A man is more forward, stronger and more vocal in his approach. A woman is more demure, using body language, and being less vocal than the man.

Rachel A. 33
Vanvouver, WA

Women approaching a man means that she is not afraid to go after what she wants. Men approaching a woman means that he is strong. There is no real difference.

Cicely B 26
Savannah, GA

There doesn't seem to be any difference. But ask a woman and she will tell you that it shows that a woman is bold and not afraid to go after what she wants and/or needs.

Dingarka J. 28
Brooklyn, NY

Love for the Family

I've got problems,
I care not to say,
Keep them deep within,
Store them far away,
See I'm still young,
Shouldn't have it this hard,
Alienated,
Forgotten,
Treated like dirt,
But that's my family,
And no one loves them,
More than me,
Would die for all of them,
Give each my last breath,
It shouldn't be this hard,
Shouldn't have to face this alone,
But it is,
And I am,
Wheres my family now,   ·
Where,
When I need them most,
They take,
never give,
Want,
But don't offer,
Shouldn't be this hard,
Shouldn't have to face this alone,
But that's my family,
And no one loves them,
More than me.

What Defines a Good Woman?

A good woman is not defined. There are good woman everywhere in this world who are as different as night and day. Mother Teresa is a great woman, but so is my mom.

Rachel A. 33
Vancouver, WA

Knowing how to carry herself like a lady at all times.

Joey S. 24
Jackson, MS

A good woman is someone who is honest to their mate. If she is honest and truthful then everything will come together

Queneshia S. 19
Athens, GA

A woman who knows her self worth and understands her unique place in the world. She also has a good understanding of her gifts in the relationship.

Unknown Female

This question can be answered in report format. But the definition of a good woman shifts depending upon the morale of the person inquiring or doing the speculation.

Day G. 25
Atlanta, GA

One who can be honest with herself and her partner. a woman that is well directed and determined.

Deneshia W. 22
Thomaston, GA

A good woman is a strong woman that isn't afraid to love and be loved. A woman that stands by her man and family through good times and bad. A woman who stimulates her equal, mentally and emotionally.

Unknown Female 24

A great woman displays her strengths, her character, and her willingness to accept a man even for his flaws.

Cicely B. 26
Savannah, GA

The definition of a good woman is somebody supportive and lifts her man up. She is someone that will do anything it takes to keep her man happy.

Erica C. 19
Atlanta, GA

Soul Searching

In the cool morning,
Watching the wind blow,
Catching natures scent,
As it surrounds my mind,
Like a child,
I want to spread my wings and fly,
Fly far far away,
To the farthest parts of my soul,
To the deepest crevases of the heart,
All I want,
Is to feel,
Taste,
What life truly is,
What the world has in store,
So let the imagination,
Run as wild as the stallions,
As free as the rainfall,
Let my imagination touch me,
In ways never experienced,
Touch me,
Till my whole world,
Is a new page turned,
I'm like a child,
Just wanting to spread my wings and fly,
Far,
Far,
Away.

Just Perfect

Grace without falter,
Something instilled in a goddess,
Elegance through humility,
A trait all hope to have,
Poise,
Perseverance,
Integrity,
And a glow,
To brighten a 1000 nights,
These are just a handful,
Of the things that make you,
Who you are,
Make you that perfect angel,
I hold every night,
That wonderful woman,
The sun rises to see,
And shines it rays,
So the world can witness you,
That very world,
Not the same,
Without you by my side,
Without me,
Waiting to see you,
In a state of utter perfection,
Its hard to be perfect,
Don't know how its done,
But some way,
Somehow,
You seem to figure it out,
My perfect angel,
Just perfect in every way.

Everything's Good

Everything in my life,
Good,
The changes made,
To turn myself,
From a child,
Into a man,
Good,
The love of my life found,
Then lost,
How could that be,
A thing so good,
A lesson learned,
My mistakes magnified,
And my punishment harsh,
So to learn through fire,
And survive the flames,
Good,
Very good,
I take the bad,
Spin it,
Twist it,
And make it a positive thing,
Everything that I have,
The changes,
The lessons learned,
Even all the mistakes made,
Are good,
Very,
Very,
Good.

What Defines a Good Working Relationship?

The Webster definition may be totally different than my own, but I think that a good working relationship is one with friendship and trust.

Kandace F. 25
San Francisco, CA

A good relationship has to have communication, prayer and the continuous lust for each other.

Dingarka J. 28
Brooklyn, NY

When two people can come together as one. When they are committed, respectful to each other. Where they take pride in each other and where they also grow together.

Jackie

If everyone is happy, then they compromise in what they want in their relationship. Also any promises that are made in their relationship are not being broken.

Cicely B. 26
Savannah, GA

To have a clear understanding and respect for each others strengths and weaknesses are what I think defines a wonderful relationship.

Unknown Female

A good working relationship is defined as a growing relationship between at least two parties where boundaries have been clearly identified and discussed. There is no room stagnation, growth, empowerment and cultivation.

Day G. 25
Atlanta, GA

My definition of a good working relationship is an open relationship where you are able to trust that other person. Also knowing that there are two people in the relationship and that everything is not about you.

Deneshia W. 22
Thomaston, GA

A good working relationship is one where two equal partners have trust, understanding, honesty, compromise, and love.

Unknown Female 22

Letter from Man

Dear God,
Its me again,
Hope you remember,
See haven't spoke,
In very long time,
But I'm in trouble now,
I need you,
Like I've always needed you,
I'm sorry,
My life in disarray,
You told me,
Told me to walk straight,
Warned me to act right,
I didn't listen,
Really didn't care,
Wanted to run my own life,
Didn't think I needed you,
See now I know,
Now I see,
That without you,
Then there is no me,
Since I was a star in the sky,
Since my very first breath,
My first cry,
You held my hand,
When I took my first steps,
But as I grew older,
My faith began to fade,
Church was an option,
Didn't even think to pray,

Only called on you,
When things went bad,
Cursed your name,
When it got even worse,
Thought I had it figured out,
Thought I was in control,
And then you showed me,
The errors of my ways,
Made me see who you really were,
Made my path,
Clear as day,
My life on a road,
Leading to chaos,
Destruction and more,
But by dropping to my knees,
And speaking to my Lord,
You gave me a new life,
A new path to follow,
Gave me something that I loved,
So God I thank you,
For being by my side,
To guide me,
Enlighten me,
To take my worries away,
But that was then,
And I'm in trouble now,
It has been awhile,
Hope you know who I am,
So here is my prayer,
Given with all the faith I can,
By the way Lord,
My name,
Man.

1000 Words

Admiration,
Affection,
Undying desire,
Just a few words to describe,
My feelings for you,
Feelings I felt,
Since the first time we met,
Not face to face,
But by picture just the same,
I noticed everything about you,
Your smile,
Your stature,
The sexy way you stared,
Captivated,
Mesmerized,
In love at first sight,
A few more words,
To show how I feel about you,
They say a picture says a 1000 words,
Tells a million tales,
But a 1000 words,
And a million tales,
Are not nearly enough,
To fully,
Describe you.

Crossroads

We're at a crossroads,
We can go east or west,
Which ever we deem the best,
But both seem hard,
Looks like there are mountains to climb,
Nothing straight,
Nothing clear,
But bumpy and curved,
Strong winds,
And fierce rains,
Making visibility on life,
Slim,
To none,
Or we could go north,
Sun shining,
Grass green,
Birds in beautiful harmony,
Seems safe,
And bright,
Any other way just couldn't be right,
Or to the south we go,
Back through the trouble,
The pain,
The utter hell of the past,
Our life's long trials,
Cant run from our past,
Can't hide from its grip,
So we look to the east,
And glance to the west,
Remember the south,

And prayed for help,
Our life at a crossroads,
But our direction now found,
To the north we travel,
This life now,
On solid ground.

Scars

There was a reason you stayed,
So now there's a reason you're gone,
I didn't push you away,
You left on your own,
Said that I had some problems,
And you didn't want any drama,
Said that I should be a man,
Because you wasn't my mother,
I tried to be the man,
You needed me to be,
I did this,
Tried that,
It wasn't me,
Now were not even friends,
Don't talk anymore,
We had something great,
Something we each,
Never had before,
But now its all just a memory,
All bad at that,
All the good times erased,
Leaving nothing but hate,
See I loved what we were,
I hate what we are,
For the way we left things,
Will leave nothing but scars.

Perfect Goddess

Today I thought only of you,
Last night I felt you in my dreams,
But soon,
I hope to find you in my kiss,
I hope to make you mine,
No matter what is said,
Matter what we fear,
Whenever I see you,
I breath a hard breath,
I feel my heart stumble,
Whenever you are near,
My mind has no knowledge,
Of the love that I have,
Never want to say goodbye,
To such a perfect goddess,
An angel that has fallen,
Is the angel that I love,
I see you in my dreams,
I see you when you are not there,
All I can do,
Is close my eyes,
And run my fingers through your hair,
Will you surrender,
To the love that has me conquered,
Can you know the way I care for you,
Every minute of every hour,
And every hour of my life,
I want you to see,
Feel,
And know,

That I am yours,
My goddess,
My perfect,
Perfect,
Goddess.

What Does a Man's Soul Consist Of?

A man's soul consists of tranquility, overall support of themselves and exceeding expectations through themselves.

JaQuinnia R. 19

A man's soul consists of desires, the desire to accomplish and conquer. The desire to be able to have what he wants and be able to take care of his woman in all aspects.

Rachel A. 33
Vancouver, WA

How to treat a woman first of all. Then there is love, respect and of course there is sex.

Queneshia S. 19
Athens, GA

His soul consists of divine knowledge, strength, stability, and love in the purest form. It's the worldly influence that changes a man's mindset

Unknown Female

A man's soul is filled with GOD, determination, will power, love and ambition.

Unknown Female 25

A man's soul consist of a woman. Because without her, there would be no him.

Seneca H. 24
Orangeburg, SC

I wish that I knew, no clue on that one. I guess it consists of longing for the affection of love. But a lot do not even want to show it.

Erica C. 19
Atlanta, GA

A man's soul consist of pain, a true struggle and a light (which shows that life could and can be better).

Dingarka J. 28
Brooklyn, NY

Protection, providing for his family, and primal animal instincts (survival methods).

Cicely B. 26
Savannah, GA

Silent Love

With everyday that passes,
And every night that creeps by,
I hold a vivid memory,
Of your granderous figure,
Flowing freely in my heart,
And knocking helplessly,
At the doorway to my soul,
Its you I want,
And its me you need,
Running my fingers through your hair,
And wiping the tears from your cheeks,
So many days have you called me,
So many nights have I had you,
Dreaming of fantasies never imagined before,
Leaving imprints of emotions,
That you dare not forget,
While shaking the stars,
From the heavens above,
More amazing than a setting sun,
Lovelier than a summer's day,
You are who you are,
And I am who you need.

Shade of Emotions

The sun sits still in your eyes,
Illuminating the path to your soul,
A lovechild is born,
With emotions felt,
Far beyond the realm of reality,
But still hidden in the depths of despair,
A feeling felt,
When eyes cut like daggers into your heart,
A feeling many share,
But few truly have,
An emotion unlike happy or sad,
A heart felt,
Soul wrenching taste,
Of true happiness,
A feeling unconfirmed to modern times,
A feeling of trueness and sincerity,
An emotion filled with tragedy and sorrow,
A feeling that completes the incomplete,
And awakens dead souls,
From there premature slumber,
A time when the weary become strong,
And the mighty cower,
In the shadows of the once pitiful,
A time when minds wander,
And hearts begin to quake,
A time now is the best time,
And whenever is never happening,
A time when love has taken control,
And love is all you need.

Woman

Great is the woman,
That stole my breath from me,
Great is she,
To stop a throbbing heart from beating,
And all the while hypnotizing a lover's mind,
With her kiss,
She turned a man,
Into a child,
Letting him yearn for the flame,
She has placed upon his soul,
And searing his eyes,
With unsurpassed perfection,
I long to find that woman,
Long to experience her tempting manner,
Her seducing smile,
While wanting her through and through,
Is she the one for me,
Or is she meant for another dismal soul,
Dismal of smile,
Dismal of faith,
But truthful,
So that she will understand,
What kind of woman,
She really is.

Life's Passion

I loved you all my life,
Even before we met,
Mostly it wasn't you,
Just the thought of loving you,
The notion of being around you,
Staying by you,
Kissing you,
I never really knew it was you,
Until I stared into your eyes,
Surprised by your passion,
And ignited by your engulfing beauty your wondrous figure,
Permanently imprinted in my heart and soul,
Our destined romance,
Playing like a fantasy in my mind,
And with one kiss,
My world is turned right side up,
And you are made my wife,
My life,
My whole world,
Even before we met,
I loved you all my life.

Everything

I see those eyes,
I see those lips,
They look to good to be real,
But I just cant resist,
I see that smile,
I run my fingers through that hair,
I still cant believe,
That you are really there,
I feel the curve of your hips,
The warmth of your tongue,
My mind now wondering,
If you are that one,
Your skin so pure,
That laugh filled with grace,
Now I can put that outline,
To an elegant face,
With all the women of the past,
All the problems I was dealt,
Seeing you,
Feeling you,
Just realizing my dream,
You're that one and only,
You have to be,
That everything.

Do You Believe in Love at First Sight?

Yes, because true love should happen. It should be really strong from that first meeting.

Cicely B. 26
Savannah, GA

No I don't think so. How can you just look at someone and know that you love them? The exterior is not the only thing that you should love.

Erica C. 19
Atlanta, GA

No, not at all. I think that love at first sight is really lust. Love is deeper than just the physical.

Kandace F. 25
San Francisco, CA

Yes I do believe in love at first sight. Sometimes you can see a person and talk to them for the first time. It then seems like you have seen them before or you could see yourself with them. Or you may know right off top, that they are the one for you.

Jackie

Not love, but an attraction. There is no such thing as love at first sight.

Rachel A. 33
Vancouver, WA

Not really. Only because I want to get to know someone before I make that jump. Looks can be very deceiving.

Queneshia S. 19
Athens, GA

No, not at all. I believe that's lust or infatuation. Love takes time to develop.

Day G. 25
Atlanta, GA

No, I believe that you have to know a person before you can you them. I do however believe in lust at first sight.

Deneshia W. 22
Thomaston, GA

Be

To be that hero,
Even in your own mind,
Gives you confidence,
Security,
An instant power-up,
You're a god,
A mountain,
The biggest of us all,
We stand tall and upright,
And still fall short of you,
So play that hero,
Be whoever you want,
Be a spy,
Be a ghost,
Haunting every house and home,
Be a star in the sky,
Or a star upon the stage,
Just be something,
Never be nothing at all,
We are all somebody,
Maybe even if its ourselves,
But be true,
Be strong,
Let nothing hold you down,
So be whoever you are,
Even in your mind,
Just be.

Photo

I see you and I wish,
You were right here with me,
I see you and I wish,
You were nowhere but here,
You're not miles and miles away,
But still so far from my open arms,
We talk,
We laugh,
But still I cant help but cry,
I've been missing you,
Yet I kiss you every night,
I have yearned for you,
Even though you sleep by my side,
I want you here,
Need you now,
My heart aching,
My soul searching,
For that answer to all my screams,
Its not the same thing,
Not the same at all,
I need you to heal my heart,
But until that day,
I still have,
Your photo.

Pain

A rabid feeling,
An astonishing ailment,
An illness,
That will not cease,
Just phrases to describe,
Words to paint with,
The canvas,
A blank soul,
The finished product,
A crushed heart,
A life no longer wanted,
An imminent death,
Not a physical demise,
But an emotional torture,
And emotion no one would desire,
Even on their worst of foes,
Utter helplessness,
Complete chaos,
A feeling felt,
But not deserved,
Deserved by no one,
But shared by man,
Shared by woman,
Even by boy and girl,
The canvas,
A blank soul,
The finished product,
A man,
Filled with pain.

My Apologies

I'm truly sorry,
For whatever I've done,
From lying,
To cheating,
Even things I just thought,
But we're meant to be,
Something I've wanted all my life,
Since our very first kiss,
Things were going to be just right,
That's why I'm sorry,
Didn't see my faults,
Thought I was perfect,
Now I see I'm not,
But what you saw,
Were two of me,
Yes a Jekyll,
And a Hyde,
I thought better to keep you guessing,
Thought better to live a lie,
My whole life was you,
Still cant get you out my mind,
From that first conversation,
Knew you were one of a kind,
Thinking of how to say,
What needs to be said,
But its hard to get over,
That you wish we never met,
My whole world was rocked,
My life now void,
The day you spoke,

And said you were gone,
It shouldn't have been like that,
You should still be with me,
Our days getting longer,
Our love getting stronger,
And that's why I'm sorry,
Why I just wish this to end,
To turn back the hands of time,
And start all over again,
To the beginning,
Yes,
All over again.

What Is True Love?

Loving someone unconditionally. Having the security that that person will love you no matter what happens.

Deneshia W. 22
Thomaston, GA

True Love. I really don't think that there is a written definition of what this is. It's really how you as an individual feels for your partner.

Unknown Female 25

True love- is that unconditional, undying, everlasting love that allows two people to unite in unison.

Seneca H. 24
Orangeburg, SC

True love to me is the willingness to put yourself on the line through anything and everything.

JaQuinnia R. 19

True love happens when there is a mutual respect, mutual admiration and cooperation, even when there are disagreements. There is also the ability to meet somewhere in the middle. You must be friends with the person that you are in love with. Lust helps a little too!

Rachel A. 33
Vancouver, WA

True love is one of those heart and mind things. One of those I will do anything feelings.

Erica C. 19
Atlanta, GA

When two people connect on more than the physical, mental and spiritual. When you generally and genuinely care about a person's well being.

Kandace F. 25
San Francisco, CA

25—35 years down the line, the family ties are not broken, the love is still there and you as a family still place God first before anything else.

Dingarka J. 28
Brooklyn, NY

When you can't breathe, live, love, smile or laugh without that person. True love is happiness, honesty, truth, respect and commitment.

Jackie

I Cry

I cry,
When I cant hold you,
I cry,
When I wake up,
And you are nowhere near me,
I cry,
Because I cant love you,
Cant love you,
Everyday of our lives,
Cant care for you,
Cant be there,
Just near you,
Ever so close,
Close enough,
To smell the sweetness of your kiss,
To taste the nectar,
Which is you,
All of you,
Everything about you,
So I can cry,
When I cant hold you,
Yes I cry,
When I wake up,
You are no where near me,
But mainly I cry because I cant love you,
Cant love you,
Everyday of our lives.

Lover or Friend

So confusing,
Don't know where I stand,
Am I your lover,
Or just your friend,
Don't keep playing this game,
All the clues make me think,
That its more than a game,
More than a relationship we had,
A friendship we've had for years,
Through all the good times,
Throughout the bad,
Through all our tears,
We've been there,
Me as your friend,
The one you call,
In the early morning hours,
But lately the game has changed,
Has gone from one entity,
To another different thing,
Our feelings have grown,
The emotions overwhelming,
Me jealous,
You suspicious,
If you're not with me,
Then you're not with them,
Cant believe its like this,
Why not keep it the same,
This relationship so confusing,
Don't know where I stand,
Am I your lover,

Or just a friend,
The nights together,
The long talks we have,
Even to the walks in the park,
Just two friends spending the day as one,
Or a new found love,
Just being born,
See my heart says one thing,
But my soul wants you to be,
My one great romance,
That one great love for me,
But its not what I want,
Not at all my call,
Are we just two friends,
Or a little more after all,
Right now so confused,
Don't know where I stand,
Am I just a friend,
Or now your man.

Fantasy

Awoke last night,
To a song in the air,
Opened my eyes,
And you were standing right there,
Your body so perfect,
Sp elegant,
Just had to have you right then,
Had to kiss you,
From head to toe,
From fingertip to fingertip,
Making sure I kissed,
Each and every inch,
My tongue searching,
Finding,
Every spot that needed me,
Your body so soft,
Just teasing me,
To the edge of insanity,
Tempting me,
Calling me,
And yes I answered,
Answered the screams of your soul,
The yearns of my body,
And you respond to me,
As I entered your innocence,
And released your mind,
With everything I have,
Your every man's dream come true,
My only reality,
The star of my fantasy.

Love

Unexplained,
Confusing,
That one person,
That one time,
Something that is earned,
Not just given,
Not just taken,
Real,
True,
Great beyond anything ever experienced,
A time when a kiss,
Is more than a kiss,
And words mean so much more,
Where a stare can create passion,
When the movements of your lips,
Mesmerize the others soul,
Hypnotizes their body,
And heaven is here on earth,
It may be unexplained,
Sometimes so confusing,
But when that time comes,
Its realer than real,
And in its truest form,
Its once in a lifetime,
And wanted by all,
Its LOVE,
Real,
True,
Unconditional L-O-V-E.

Always Working

I'm always working,
To bring you into my life,
You are joy,
You're pain,
You're sunshine,
After the rain,
You're misery,
A miracle,
The one who makes me cry,
My world,
My downfall,
Hell,
You're the apple of my eye,
So much to me,
The completion of my soul,
The right to my left,
The ying to my yang,
Even a renewed life,
To my long suffering death,
A breath of fresh air,
To fill my shriveled lungs,
That's why I do what I do,
Work as hard as I can,
To bring you into my life,
To make me a better man.

The Best Man

I'm better than most,
Maybe the best you've ever seen,
I'm the man that you wish for,
You know I'm the man of your dreams,
I have everything,
All rolled into one,
Intelligence,
Attractiveness,
Dangerous,
Like a loaded gun,
Accomplished,
But still hungry,
Always ready to eat,
Well dressed,
Well liked,
All I can say is well done,
So when you look at me,
You cant roll your eyes,
You'll have to stand there,
Mesmerized,
Just stare for awhile,
I'm better than most,
Yeah that's me,
Maybe the best you've ever seen,
I'm the man that you wish for,
I'm that man in your dreams.

Short and Sweet

I read something earlier,
And it made me think of you,
It had me tearing,
Had me thinking,
My heart beating a million times,
All my emotions coming through,
It was deeper than love itself,
Had the insight,
Of a thousand Buddhas,
It was history that hadn't happened yet,
It was faith,
All depending upon you,
The key to my universe,
The keeper of my soul,
What I read,
Defied gravity,
And rewrote,
The chapters of my life,
The words on that page,
Could baffle the greatest of minds,
The keenest of scientists,
And the most romantic of them all,
See what I read,
Was just that deep,
The length was barely a page,
Just right to describe you,
What I read,
Was short and sweet.

Falling Rain

I have to see you,
You're in everything I do,
You're everywhere I go,
And wherever I look,
You seem to be right there,
I cant do this,
I cant love a ghost,
Love a woman that is gone from my sight,
I cant love a woman,
That is gone from my life,
You could have stayed,
But you chose to leave,
Broke all the promises you made,
To satisfy your ego,
To say it was me,
Made you look like a fool,
You ran from love,
Chased away me and you,
So I cant do this,
Cant love you anymore,
My greatest love,
Also my greatest lose,
But that is what you are,
Lost,
Lost from my touch,
My kiss,
Lost from my world,
As hard as this is,
Its even harder for me,
I wanted to give you,

Everything you dreamed,
A life of happiness,
A house,
With that white picket fence,
But I won't love you anymore,
You're no longer real to me,
A figment of my imagination,
A ghost of the past indeed,
So I cant love you,
Won't love you,
Won't subject myself to such pain,
But I will remember us,
With every drop of the rain.

Anticipation

When you want something so bad,
You can taste it in the air,
When you feel it so much,
You wish it was right there,
I anticipate you being here,
Long to spend my life with you,
Anticipate you being my wife,
Being the biggest,
Brightest,
Part of my life,
You're a joy to be with,
An angel from the stars,
An anticipation felt,
Long before you were known,
I cant believe you're here,
Anticipated a life of loneliness,
But you entered my life,
Changed my whole point of view,
Anticipated I fall in love,
Once my eyes saw you,
You're everything to me,
The biggest,
Brightest,
Part of my life,
Just never thought,
I could anticipate you,
Being my wife.

My Friend

I try to be,
Who you want to be,
Not let emotions grab my soul,
Pierce my heart,
And take control,
Trying to be that friend,
You so desperately need,
Yes,
Trying to be that friend indeed,
My whole world is in your hands,
My life now revolves around you,
Savoring every moment shared,
Conquering all the feelings felt,
I lay in bed,
And think of you,
Dream of you,
Let my imagination unfold,
Then I look to my left,
And you are right there with me,
But as a friend,
And only a friend,
A beautiful butterfly,
Whose hands hold my world,
A child masquerading as a man,
My friend,
Only my friend.

Young Thing

A little younger than most,
But still able to be a man's man,
True to form,
True to my heart,
Myself,
Never pressured,
Nor influenced,
About my own values,
And beliefs,
So yes I'm a young thing,
Still a man's man,
Letting bad turn to good,
Allowing good to be great,
My life just beginning,
Just starting to take off,
Ready for a trip,
To the furthest reaches of my soul,
To learn,
Explore,
To grow,
Become the mentor and scholar,
That I am supposed to be,
This responsibility,
This life mine for the taking,
Never pressured,
Nor influenced,
Even though,
I'm still a young thing.

Can All Problems in a Relationship Be Worked out for the Better?

Most problems yes, but not all problems. It takes two to make it better.

Jackie

Yes of course they can. It wouldn't be a relationship if you couldn't work them out.

Cicely B. 26
Savannah, GA

No, sometimes you get into a relationship you shouldn't have been in. You can just shut up and deal with it, but most times you just have to let it go.

Erica C. 19
Atlanta, GA

If both parties are willing to work it out, they can solve their problems. But if one isn't willing to meet at least halfway, then they as a couple will never be able to completely resolve their issues.

Rachel A. 33
Vancouver, WA

Depends on what the problem is. They can be worked out, but if they become repetitive, then there is no reason to try and work them out.

Deneshia W. 22
Thomaston, GA

Yes they can. Helps the relationship grow. Also let's the couple learn the flaws and imperfections of the other party in the relationship.

Queneshia S. 19
Athens, GA

Got My Eyes on You

Seen you from across the room,
My gaze focused only on you,
You're a muse,
An inspiration,
You're magic in the air,
When I look at you,
My slight glance,
Becomes a transient stare,
I imagine nervous emotions,
Becoming seductive words,
Imagine a shy demeanor,
Becoming a passionate kiss,
I'm a witness,
To your beauty,
Both inside and out,
I'm a player to your game,
Not a rookie,
But a pro,
Eye contact just waiting to happen,
The avoidance you give,
Just teasing my soul,
I've got a jones,
And only a taste of you,
Can satisfy my urge,
I put my imagination in check,
And release myself from my seat,
Step by step,
Hard breath by breath,
I see your figure,
See that elegant frame,

That smile to lighten the world,
Those eyes to captivate,
Any and every universe,
I see everything I want,
But its you I pass,
To nervous to share my feelings,
To sprung to let my guard down,
I cant open my heart,
Not so soon,
But until I can,
Hope you know,
I got my eyes on you.

Just You

You're an explorer,
Searching the depths,
Finding your treasures,
You're an architect,
Building the bridges,
Connecting the unconnected,
You're a rambler,
Never stable,
Never settling,
Where the wind blows you,
That is home,
You search,
You build,
You fly from place to place,
But you're a man,
A woman,
A boy or girl,
Whatever you are,
You're a part of me,
A part of us,
A race,
A creed,
A sex,
An age,
No discrimination,
Just discipline,
Just you.

Crazy in Love

I'm going insane,
Deranged,
Losing my mind over you,
Said I love you in just days,
Doing things in months,
When a longer time it should take,
I fall hard in love,
Don't know why,
Or how,
Just know what I want,
What I need,
Someone to kiss,
That one woman to hold,
The more time we share,
The more our love shows,
Its true,
Its right,
Perfect in every possible way,
I just think its to soon,
My heart never beating so fast,
With one long stare,
Your eyes erasing every heartache in my past,
So I see why I'm going insane,
Have lost my mind over you,
I'm head over heels crazy,
Crazy in love with you.

You and I

You and I,
We're so destined to be,
One entity,
One soul,
One heart that beats,
Were two of a kind,
You and I,
A long love coming,
Generations forming,
Forever being loved,
Never being neglected,
My life,
My blood,
My very last breath,
You and I,
Something that I have long been looking for,
Me and you,
Us and them,
Nothing,
Not nothing,
Compares to the sound,
The passion,
The unconditional love that's shared,
Between you and I.

What I Give

What I give,
To make you mine,
My heart,
My soul,
My body and time,
I'll give you the sun,
The stars,
The moon and the clouds,
I'll give you everything,
And nothing les,
I'll give you the air in my lungs,
I'll give you my life,
Just want to give you,
Everything that I can,
See I'm that man,
That loves to give,
More than he receives,
Not that man,
That takes,
And lets be,
So whatever you want,
Is what I'll give,
To make you smile,
And what I'll give to you,
Is all my life.

Average Joe

Just an average man,
With a big heart,
Your average person,
With a soul of gold,
Just that average guy,
That you barely know,
I'm nobody special,
Just your average Joe,
Walking tall,
On just an average day,
Still just average,
No matter what they say,
I'm everything average,
Just bigger than life,
A small man,
On an incredible high,
Just an average guy,
An average man,
Just as normal as you or them,
No name,
Just a smile,
Sometimes,
Just a him,
So I'm that guy,
That you may never know,
I'm nobody special,
Just your average Joe.

Starlite

Starlite,
Star bright,
As I look towards the stars tonight,
I wish I may,
Just wish I might,
Be with you,
For the rest of my life,
With eyes shining,
Like those very same stars,
Brighter than diamonds,
Just like the one you are,
That someone special,
My one lost love,
365,
12,
And 24,
Measurements that dictate,
That great relationship,
So starlite,
Star bright,
First star I see tonight,
I wish it may,
I wish it might,
Grant my wish,
To have you as my wife.

Not Ready

I'm not ready to let you go,
Not ready to let you leave,
Don't see how,
You can just turn your back,
And walk away from me,
I don't know what I did,
So I'll grab my coat,
And chase you halfway down the street,
 Cause my hearts not ready to let you go,
And my soul just cant let you leave,
I put all my feelings,
Into everything I've done,
I've laid all my emotions,
On my sleeve to see,
Did it so you can see,
Just how I felt,
How I am,
Did it,
Because I wanted you to know,
That I was true,
So I'm not ready to end this,
This,
What I have dreamed about my entire life,
But for it to slip through the cracks,
My light,
Transforming back into the dark,
I'm not ready to let you go,
Not ready to let you leave,
Don't see how,
You can just turn your back,
And walk away from me.

Inspiration

My inspirations gone,
She just went away,
No eyes,
No smile,
No more perfect shape,
My inspirations gone,
Just took her love away,
She was my muse,
My thoughts,
She was the words I wrote,
She was everything to me,
She made my soul breath,
She made my heart beat,
But now she gone,
Don't know where she went,
Was she called back to heaven,
For an angel sent she was,
Or is she wandering around,
Breathing life into a dead world,
My inspirations gone,
She just went away,
No last hug to remember,
No kiss goodbye,
My inspirations gone,
Just took her love away.

Stay the Night

It was such a great time,
Didn't want it to end,
A special day,
With a special lady,
The time flashed past,
The morning coming fast,
Didn't want it to end,
Didn't want you to go,
All I wanted,
Was for you,
To stay the night,
We both lost track of time,
Less of your fault,
More of mine,
I didn't want you to go,
Wanted to wake with you,
Right there by my side,
It was just so right,
The stars shining,
The moon full,
Our bodies conversing as one,
Just wish you had,
Still wish you would,
Maybe one of theses times,
Think about it,
And maybe you just might,
Come over with me,
And stay the night.

Chariety

She's my dream come true,
She's my road less traveled,
My perfect rose,
My day of sun,
After that thunderous rain,
She's a diamond in the rough,
That twinkle in the sky,
She's one in a million,
She's a fantasy turned reality,
She's a yes to everyone's no,
She's that silhouette in blinding light,
She's that woman in my bed at night,
The mother of my seed,
The producer of my affection,
She's the reason for my struggles,
The reason for my pain,
She's the reason I strive so hard,
She's the reason I never say cant,
She's the first thought I think,
The last person I see,
She's everything I want,
Everything I need,
She's everything I am,
My whole entire world,
She's my life,
My chosen one,
She knows,
She's my Chariety.

Crying Times

With one look in your eyes,
And a break of my heart,
I knew I had made you cry,
I didn't want to see your tears,
Didn't want to know your hurt,
But they came,
Came like thunder during the storm,
Each one striking deeper into my soul,
Until that moment,
That one moment which bonded woman and man,
Like the leaves to a tree,
That single moment,
Sealed a romance for eternity,
Gave new measure to our love,
And gave both our hearts,
A gaze into each others soul,
It was a time,
When all our strengths,
Combined to be just enough,
To hold one another,
Me comforting you,
As you consoled me,
That one moment frozen in our minds,
As we made love,
Until the song of the birds,
That one moment,
When I cried with you.

Are We Still There

We were once in a place,
Where relationships take shape,
And love conquers all,
We were once in a place,
Where we called each other,
Saw each other,
And thought about each other,
We were once in a place,
Where we thought we would always be,
Thought we would always stay,
But lately I don't know,
Are we still there,
Are we still on that same page,
Still singing that same note,
I want to know,
Are we still in each others life,
Are we still thinking,
About what the others doing,
What the others feeling,
If the other is thinking about us,
I'm trying to find the words,
To say what I'm feeling,
To express what I want,
But all I want to say,
And all I need to know,
Is are we still there.

Love You

I cant take this much longer,
Its killing me inside,
Feeling a pain like never before,
Emotions that I not experienced,
You make me,
You complete me,
You know you're everything to me,
But I cant take this pain,
You say you're not mad,
Say you're not hurt,
Just little things I did,
Made you take this joy from me,
Its crazy that you haven't called,
Crazy that we don't talk at all,
We spent the beginning of us,
Trying to stay in touch,
But my patience is wearing thin,
This hurt getting stronger,
I'm losing it,
Hope I'm not losing you,
My mind confused,
My heart ceasing to beat,
And my soul,
Feeling like it has lost its best friend,
We can still make this work,
We can still make us happen,
To take away this pain,
To make me feel whole again,
New once again,
Our relationship like a new page,

Able to scribe a new beginning,
A wonderful story,
And a fairy tale end,
All I want to do is love you,
Adore you,
Make you happy,
Beyond anything you've felt,
I deserve you,
And we deserve us,
But I cant take this much longer,
Its killing me inside,
Feeling a pain like never before,
Having emotions I have not experienced,
I love you,
Cant help but love you,
Because all I want to do,
Is love you.

Have You Ever Been in a Committed Relationship?

Of course I have! I prefer to be in a committed relationship rather than "playing the field." I enjoy being with the same man in a committed relationship where neither party even wants to cheat on the other.

Rachel A. 33
Vancouver, WA

Yes and no. The perception changes with time. At the time I thought I was in love, but now with time and hindsight your definition of love and what type of relationship you were in changes.

Stacy M. 30-something
Providence, RI

Yes I believe in commitment. I knew he was committed to me, so I tried it out with him and I liked it. During that commitment, I found someone who loves me for me and respected me as a woman and a person.

Jackie

Yes I have been in a committed relationship. As a matter of fact I was married. He gave me what I needed. I was comfortable, it felt right, it felt really good.

Cicely B. 26
Savannah, GA

Yes, they had something to offer me that would work well for the both of us in a committed relationship.

Erica C. 19
Atlanta, GA

I've been in a committed relationship and I believe in the connection between a man and a woman that can only be achieved through a relationship that is more than just a friendship.

Unknown Female

My Heart

My heart,
The life blood of romance,
The device that breathes life,
Into everything in me,
Around me,
And for you,
You take my heart,
Cherish it,
Caress it,
Treat it like the flower that it is,
I give this to you,
For I know you want it,
Adore it,
Yearn to occupy its vacant space,
Without you,
Its cold,
Its dark,
My heart is dead,
To the world outside of you,
My heart without you,
Is like a storm without rain,
A kiss without passion,
It can happen,
But its rare and seldom seen,
You without my heart,
Is something that frightens me,
Scares me to the core,
Makes my mind wander,
My soul weep,
You are where my heart belongs,
Longs to stay,
My heart attached to you,

Cries for you,
My heart just waiting for you,
I give you my heart,
Its love,
Honor,
Its valor,
Its sincerity,
I give you my heart,
Its honesty,
Humility,
Its compassion,
Its remorse,
I give you my heart,
Its forgiveness,
Respect,
Its regrets,
Its secrets,
I give you my heart,
The one thing,
I'm scared to share,
But you,
I'm scared to lose,
So with all my love,
Affection,
With everything that I am,
I give you me,
Give you my body,
My grace,
Give you the soul of this man,
In this box,
I give you all my love,
Right now,
I give you,
My heart.

To You with Love

On this day,
Those wonderful years ago,
In front of God,
Family,
And friends,
With elegance and grace,
I gave you my heart,
My soul,
My unconditional love,
On this day,
I gave you all of me,
Since that day,
My love has grown,
To bounds past eternity,
To limits that cannot be imagined,
Our two souls joined,
To become one heart,
You have become my universe,
My life,
I am your husband,
And I am so proud,
That you are my wife,
You're the beginning to my day,
The end to my night,
You take away my wrongs,
Because your everything that's right,
You're that missing piece,
To an incomplete puzzle,
That thunderous rain,
To feed a hundred year drought,

So today I have to say thank you,
From the deepest depths of my soul,
For God sent me an angel,
Who he knows I adore,
So lets celebrate today,
Because its one of many more,
Many more days of us as one,
Many more nights of me holding you,
My arms protecting you,
From all the worlds harms,
On this day,
A day in which lives are made for,
I kiss you,
Like its our first kiss,
I hold you,
Like its our last,
Look forward to the future,
And remember all the good from the past,
So when we lay down,
And I kiss you good night,
I'll be there beside you,
And I'll love you,
Every second,
Of every minute,
Every day,
For the rest of our lives.

You Don't Know Me

You don't know me,
You never did,
When you kissed me,
You were kissing a stranger,
Every time you held me,
You were holding a ghost,
Never knew what I liked,
Never knew who I really was,
I loved you,
And you gave me emptiness,
Just adored you,
And you looked right through me,
Looked through all,
I wanted to share with you,
I tried to blind you with passion,
I tried to open your heart,
Open your soul,
Wanted to open your eyes,
To a man that cared about you,
Cared about your life,
Cared about all that concerned you,
I wanted to open your eyes to me,
To a real man,
But you didn't want to love me,
Didn't want to see me,
So you hurt me,
Just because,
You didn't know me.

Journey

By train,
By plane,
Or even by the gaze of your eyes,
Take that journey,
To the very depths of my soul,
Go to a place,
Not every woman dares to go,
I want you to know me,
Want you to love me,
All my secrets hidden,
Locked away,
Deep in my souls being,
I want you inside my mind,
Deeper inside my heart,
I want you to hold my hand,
And take that journey with me,
Let me guide you,
Enlighten you,
Show you what I am all about,
So whatever you think,
Whatever's on your mind,
Let me be there,
Let me know,
I want to know you,
Want to love you,
So by the gaze of your eyes,
Take that journey,
To the very depths of my soul.

Lady

You're more than who you are,
You're every man's dream,
Mere reality turned fantasy,
Pure rain on a lover's lips,
You're not just that girl,
Or the woman next door,
You're that honey in the morning,
That twinkle in my eye,
That gift under the tree,
After waiting all that night,
Its dangerous to say,
But I think I'm so in love,
Not with you,
But everything that you are,
I wait to see you,
Even when you are standing right there,
So be rain on this lover's lips,
My beautiful fantasy,
Turned absolute reality
Be my star,
My sun,
My entire universe,
You're not just that girl,
Or that woman next door,
You're my gift under the tree,
You're that lady I adore.

My Name

I'm known throughout the world,
Known in every country,
I'm known to every race,
I live in everything,
In every smile,
I'm in every face,
I hold the key to pure happiness,
I'm the thing that's hard to hold,
I'm a kiss,
A hug,
A long look in her eyes,
I have a name that signifies total joy,
I have a name that gives,
Doesn't take,
And is exactly what you deserve,
I'm everywhere you look,
I'm every time you breath,
I'm anything you want,
I'm that thing you need,
Yes I'm here,
To give you all you desire,
From dreams,
To fantasies,
And to that just reality,
So just in case,
By now you don't know,
For all who believe,
My name is love.

To You, Is Sex as Important as Trust in a Relationship?

Sex is very, very important to me. And why wouldn't it be. It is something that is so sacred and so misunderstood. Also at times it can be very overrated, and so is trust in a relationship.

Unknown Female

Intimacy is as important as trust, sex is not. And we all know that sex and intimacy are two totally different things.

Unknown Female

I believe that sex should definitely be sacred between two adults (only marriage). It's thought of as the most expressive form of trust and/or intimacy. Unfortunately, people want to get intimate at the introduction stage of a relationship, which can get pretty complicated and can create permanent outcomes to temporary feelings.

Day G. 25
Atlanta, GA

Sometimes it may just be the initial attraction to a person. It depends on the relationship, but still sex is not as important as trust.

Deneshia W. 22
Thomaston, GA

No I do not think sex is as important as trust in any relationship. The most important reason for that is that trust is the basic foundation in a relationship. Without that trust, you don't have anything.

Seneca H. 24
Orangeburg, SC

No sex isn't that important. Because without trust there is no relationship. Why have sex with a person who you do not trust?

Queneshia S. 19
Athens, GA

No, trust is more important, and trust deeply affects your sex life. The more trust there is, the more sex there is. Also the less inhibited sex will come with the most trust.

Rachel A. 33
Vancouver, WA

No I don't think that sex is as important to the trust factor in a relationship. The trust is what makes the relationship last longer and less complicated.

Dingarka J. 28
Brooklyn, NY

Trust is a emotion that is based on a relationship. Where the sex part is just a small part of the relationship. So my answer is no, I don't think that sex is anywhere close to being as important as trust in the relationship.

Jackie

Yes sex is as important as trust. If you do not have good sex, then I will be faking everything including the trust in the relationship.

Cicely B. 26
Savannah, GA

No I don't see sex as being as important as trust in any of my relationships. Trust is much more important than sex, you may not even have sex, let alone make love, if you don't trust one another.

Erica C. 19
Atlanta, GA

No since trust should be there way before you have sex with that person. You need to have the trust in the relationship before you try and have the sex there.

Kandace F. 25
San Francisco, CA

Free Spirit

I'm a free spirit,
No chains on my wrists,
No shackles on my feet,
I'm a free spirit,
A mind that wonders,
A mouth that speaks,
A heart that beats,
And eyes that see,
I'm a free spirit,
Able to touch the heavens,
With a single kiss,
To soar to the galaxy,
Reaching each and every star,
I'm a free spirit,
So I'm free to live,
I'm a free spirit,
With the right to love,
Just the right to life,
To strive,
Struggle,
To overcome,
I'm a free spirit,
No chains on my wrists,
No shackles on my feet,
Able to touch the heavens,
With a single kiss.

Can't Wait

I understand the situation,
Still new to one another,
Cant rush,
But cant wait,
Want to be as much to you as possible,
Just don't want to speak to soon,
Don't want to seem to sprung,
So helplessly in love,
But that's just it,
And that's really what I am,
Felt like this,
From the very first gaze,
But I wont rush,
But I still cant wait,
Want to hold you,
Want to love you,
All I want to do is serve you,
That is what you deserve,
And that is what I'll give,
You want what I can hand you,
And still I'll give you more,
But I wont rush,
And still I cant wait,
Cant wait to kiss you,
Cant wait to be apart of your life,
Our dreams,
Our reality,
All cut from the same cloth,
We're two in one,
The same in taste,

The same in light,
that's what I see,
that's what I like,
And still I wont rush,
And still I cant wait,
So I'm looking forward to that chance,
To make two lives so complete,
See I'm looking to make you happy,
Beyond anything and everything,
To make you happy beyond belief,
So come here now,
Come to me to adore,
Because I will not rush,
But I will not wait.

Lost Without Love

Are there any winners,
When love goes wrong,
You've been happy,
The love is strong,
And you've meant it for so long,
There cant be any winners,
Because all the love is lost,
There cant be any winners,
Just look at what it cost,
Heartache,
Pain,
So many years of your life,
So are there any winners,
When love has gone,
The love has went away,
There's no winners,
As far as I can see,
Not her,
Not him,
Not us,
Not me,
Just hurt,
And anger,
Is all you get,
When love goes wrong.

Second Chance

Didn't think I would get it,
But I did,
Never thought I would hold you again,
But I am,
I thought,
We were over,
But we're not,
I got a rarity in life,
A second chance,
A second chance at loving you,
A continuation from our start,
It was so hard without you,
But I did struggle on,
With my thoughts of us,
My images of you,
And your voice,
Always singing in my ear,
I was hoping to see you,
And my dream came true,
I was longing to tease you,
And now that time has come,
My time,
Our time,
The hour of our love revealed,
Didn't think I would get it,
But now I did,
I got a rarity in life,
I got a second chance,
A second chance at loving you.

Baby Magic

We're having a baby,
So much fear in your heart,
So many confusing thoughts in your mind,
And still so much love in your soul,
this was not to happen,
but it was so meant to be,
just by chance,
it was you and me,
by the grace of God,
we are now mom and dad,
we're having a baby,
so proud of it am I,
my wildest dream come true,
wishful thinking made real,
but darkness surrounds us,
hatred engulfing your soul,
I'm missing priceless moments,
losing precious time,
I want to be,
what a good man should be,
that provider for his family,
a husband to his wife,
a wonderful father to his child,
we're having a baby,
and I am so pleased that it is you,
this was not to happen,
but it was so destined to be,
and just by chance,
it was me and you,
and by the grace of God,
you and,
have turned into,
mom and dad.

Stronger than Love

People say I'm this,
knowing I am more of that,
what people think,
has little effect on who I am,
but what you say,
and how you think,
means all the world to me,
when I see your face,
I light up with joy,
when I see your smile,
my life then has meaning,
and when you as that woman,
move your lips,
just to speak a word,
gives me an energy,
only God should bestow,
you're what I wake up for,
what I sleep for,
I am so in love with you,
no idea of it,
no second thoughts,
just the fine art of falling in love,
this art never to be perfected,
just practiced,
practiced,
until you meet that angel,
take her hand,
fall in love with her eyes,
her smile,
and that movement of her lips,

then and only then,
will your practice turn permanent,
and that angel become your own,
but know,
because I do,
who my angel is,
and every time I see her face,
I light up with joy,
whenever I see her smile,
my life then has meaning,
and when you as my woman,
move those captivating lips,
just to speak a single word,
I am given an energy,
a love,
that only God should bestow.

Not Supposed To

I'm going through so much,
yet a man isn't supposed to cry,
I hide my tears,
live my life,
but still,
I'm going through so much,
going through a hell like no other,
being hurt,
day in,
and wanting it to end,
day out,
life's greatest moments,
just passing me by,
love,
just a tease to me,
I'm going through a hell like no other,
still I'm not supposed to cry,
can't hide my tears any longer,
knowing that every second,
my feelings grow stronger,
I am flesh and blood,
fears and pain,
and with me going through so much,
my tears fall like the rain,
so I need my pain to end,
need my life to stop its spin,
my love to return,
and wipe these tears away,
I'm going through so much,
and a man isn't supposed to cry,

but I'm flesh and blood,
fears and pain,
knowing I'm not supposed to,
but with me going through so much,
my tears flow like the rain.

You're It

I'm changing emotions,
one reason only,
I have multiple personalities,
one reason alone,
when I change my attitude way too much,
there's one reason,
a reason that not even I can explain,
simple yet complex,
like the love I have,
for that very same reason,
they say you are who you associate with,
and my association begins,
and ends with you,
you tempt me,
tease me,
hurt me,
degrade me,
yet you ask why I change,
told you simple,
yet complex,
you may have moved on,
so why can't I,
why not shut off all emotions,
like it seems you have,
I can't stop,
maybe I won't stop,
but there's one reason,
my whole life has changed,
one reason alone,
and that reason is you,

that lone question in my life,
no other thing,
you're all that I need,
you're everything that I am.

Metaphor

Life is a race,
so many are scared to run,
so many scared to live,
thinking every step taken,
is a step closer to disaster,
a step closer to falling down,
an endless abyss of dispair,
but all races have losers,
and every race a winner,
the race of life must be run to win,
never a loser,
if the race is run right,
if the race is run with sincerity,
compassion,
run with vigor,
and strength,
never a loser,
when life is lived to it's fullest,
when obstacles are looked at,
and laughed upon,
always a winner,
when you take what life throws,
catch it,
smile,
and walk into the sunset,
life is a race,
so many are scared to run,
so many scared to live,
thinking every step taken,
is a step closer to disaster,
life is a race,
which you should run to win

Must You Have a Good Friendship, to Have a Good Working Relationship?

There has to be some sort of friendship because that is what helps in sustaining a comfort level in your relationship.

Unknown Female

Yes you do have to have a good friendship before or even during a relationship. The friendship comes with the relationship. They have to come hand in hand.

Deneshia W. 22
Thomaston, GA

I believe a good friendship is a must to a good relationship because it allows you to build a stable foundation with that person on another level.

Seneca H. 24
Orangeburg, SC

I think that you must have at least a friendship before jumping into a relationship. Some relationships start off as friendships, you do things with your mate that you would do with your friends.

Jackie

Yes, friendship should be the basis for which your relationship stands. Without a friendship, the relationship will lack trust and communication.

Stacy M. 30-something
Providence, RI

Let it Go

It's a love so good,
from the beginning,
I knew that it would,
but things grew cold,
the love got old,
and we went our separate ways,
I tossed and turned,
without you by my side at night,
missing you every second,
of every hour,
knowing that what we had,
was just so right,
but what could I do,
I had everything to say,
but no time to speak,
your eyes cut like swords,
made a child out of this man,
a cub out of a lion,
thought I was stronger than this,
thought that without you I could live,
my days grew dreary,
while my soul got sick,
knew I was stronger,
your love I tried to resist,
but from the beginning,
our love was good,
but things grew cold,
and our love got old,
and the one thing I knew,
I couldn't let go.

Until

Tonight,
I want to make love to you,
until the stars stop shining,
tonight,
let me love you,
just until,
night becomes day,
and the afternoon sun,
shines softly in your eyes,
tonight,
let me love you,
until the sheets are saturated with passion,
and the only noise to be heard,
is the deep exhales by our hearts,
tonight,
I want to love you,
no matter how long,
no matter the hours passed,
tonight,
and for all the nights to follow,
let me love you,
tonight,
if only for nothing else to happen,
let me touch you,
tease you,
please you,
tonight,
let me love you,
love you just until.

That Same Love

I look at you,
and you look at me,
in your eyes,
there is still that same love,
there's no hate,
no regrets,
just hidden,
displaced,
unconditional love,
you may spit in my face,
step on my dreams,
you may even look me right in the eyes,
and tell me you don't care,
but inside you're dying,
on the outside wanting to cry,
and the more you see me,
the more it hurts,
I'm trying to be there,
just trapped by your feelings,
those false feelings of hate,
but I'm here,
and here is where I'll stay,
because frankly,
when I look at you,
and you look at me,
our souls meet,
and we both see,
there is still,
that same love.

Valentine's Day

I wanted to hold you,
wanted to touch you,
feel you,
kiss you,
love you,
on this day,
what I wanted,
was everything you are,
you could be my gift,
my delight,
my little piece of heaven,
what I want,
see I can't have,
I can't enjoy,
on this day,
I want more than I can have,
more than you will allow,
what I want is you,
nothing more,
nothing less,
this day so special,
the day of love,
the night of passion,
on this day,
what I wanted,
was whatever you imagined,
was all our dreams to come true,
this day,
so much like every other,
so similiar,

but so unique,
a new page to be turned,
a new night to be savored,
on this day,
I wanted to be there,
wanted you to be here,
this day so special to me,
that all my thoughts were of you,
and all my day dreams,
had your smile,
on this very day,
only you would do,
only your kiss would work,
I wanted you her,
I wanted to be right there,
on this special day,
I just wanted to love you,
on this day,
Valentines Day.

Fatherhood

I didn't have a father,
not my real one,
not one that I could pretend was him,
I was alone,
to teach myself the roles of a man,
to one day be nothing like my own,
a vow I will always honor,
a promise I will never break,
to love my child,
cherish even their mistakes,
protect my blood,
and nourish their mind,
no one stepped up to play the role,
no one wanted to heed the call,
to them I was another's,
not their responsibility at all,
I won't put that burden on any man,
see I'll be right there beside my child,
on the first day of school,
be there to hold their hand,
when they awake to a nightmare,
I'll be there to kiss them goodnight,
and there to wake them to a brand new day,
on birthdays,
on holidays,
at any minute,
on any given day,
I will be there,
to bandage up cuts,
after each and every fall,

to teach them,
just as much as they will teach me,
I will be there,
no matter what I have to do,
because all I am going to be,
is the father,
no one wanted to be to me.

Printed in the United States
206889BV00003B/194/A

9 781424 114078